LÉONIE MARSH

Questions on Dressage

J. A. Allen
London

British Cataloguing in Publication Data

Marshall, Léonie M. (Léonie Mary)
  Questions on Dressage
  1. Livestock: Horses. Riding. Dressage – Manuals
  I. Title
  798.2'3

ISBN 0–85131–474–0

Published in Great Britain in 1989 by
J. A. Allen & Company Limited,
1, Lower Grosvenor Place, Buckingham Palace Road,
London, SW1W 0EL

Printed and bound in Great Britain by
WBC Ltd Bristol & Maesteg

Contents

Introduction

Over the years, beginners, novice riders trying to school their horses in basic obedience, people aspiring to ride dressage, and riders with horses with difficult problems, have asked a variety of questions regarding training.

In this book I have endeavoured to give some answers which are comprehensible and concise and all of which have been tried and proved by experts.

Reference may have to be made to textbooks regarding aids and description of exercises, etc., but the idea of this book was to give the rider a course of action to take, which he may, through lack of knowledge or experience, been unable to work out for himself.

As with all things, there is more than one route to get where you are going, but having decided upon one, stick to it, and you stand a chance of arrival!

Léonie Marshall

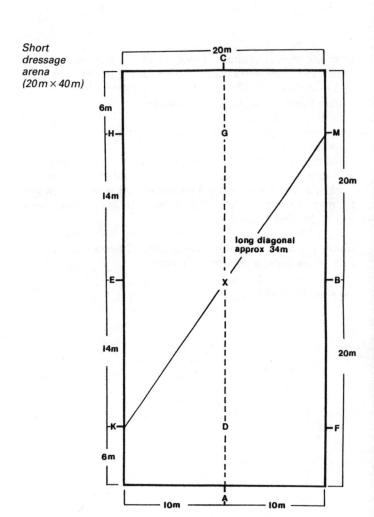

Short dressage arena (20m × 40m)

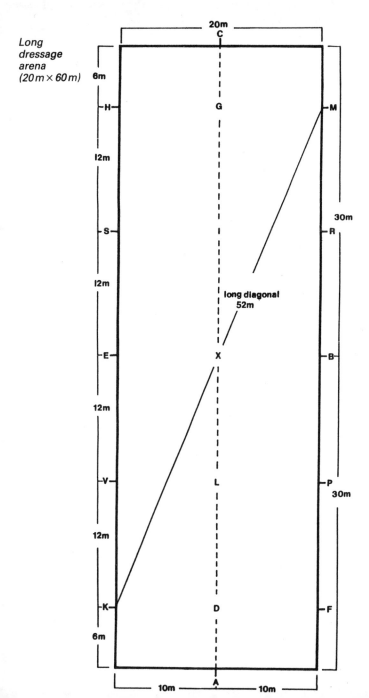

Long dressage arena (20 m × 60 m)

20m

C

6m

H — — G — — M

12m

30m

S — — R

12m

long diagonal 52m

E — — X — — B

12m

V — — P

L

30m

12m

K — — D — — F

6m

10m — A — 10m

Question: Could you advise me as to the type of horse I should buy if I want to compete in dressage competitions and do I need to have a Hanoverian?

Answer: A good deal depends on whether you desire to compete at 'the top', or whether your ambition is more modest. A 'top' horse is hard to find and expensive to buy, but there are many different varieties who can go quite a long way and give their riders considerable success. There are some general qualities which one might look for:

Head joined to neck with plenty of room to allow flexion.

Naturally cresty neck coming up out of the withers.

A short back, but not too short.

Rounded strong quarters with hind legs built underneath them.

Good bone and substance. Good length of stride and freedom of shoulders.

A slightly rounded action of the foreleg, and naturally active action of the joints of the hind legs.

Straight action is preferable, but not absolutely essential.

A willing but equable temperament is an enormous help.

Height should be decided according to the size, shape and ability of the rider. It is really no good choosing an enormous horse if the rider is only 1.37 m (4 ft 6 in), or is inclined to be plump! Nor should a novice rider choose something which may look right for the job, but which they cannot handle.

As rider and horse will probably have many years together, it is important to choose something suitable which can be enjoyed and not be exhausting or frustrating because of its unwillingness or poor temperament.

We cannot all buy the horse we would really like, but there are horses around who have a lot of ability in their way, and who, if correctly and systematically trained, will have a lot of success.

Question: I own a thoroughbred mare and she seems to become tense and over-excited, resisting in all sorts of ways at every new thing I try to teach her. Is she unsuitable for dressage?

Answer: Unfortunately without seeing her I cannot really tell you, but thoroughbreds are a law unto themselves, and a knowledge of the way they react mentally and physically is essential if one is going to try to train them. Excitability is certainly not an ideal temperament for dressage because of the difficulty in obtaining sufficient calmness for the brain to be receptive to learning.

A great deal of patience is required to train such horses, the rider having to accept the fact that it will all take a good deal longer than with a horse of equable nature.

It is impossible to train a horse, particularly for such a precise discipline as dressage, without exact control by the legs and hands of the rider. This in itself can be hard to do on a horse whose excitability leads it to nervous tension at any kind of real control. It can be done, but will certainly be a challenge, taking years rather than months.

The other factor regarding excitable horses is that of the rider, who will require a firm quiet seat and steady hands. Any looseness in the saddle, poor contact, lack of co-ordination or inconsistency of aids will upset and confuse the horse, which may result in excitability or resistance.

There are many horses who are classed as excitable or very resistant, but a good deal or all of it could be reduced by knowledge and better riding.

Question: I have a very lazy horse which I find I cannot get going. Have you any suggestions?

Answer: It is difficult to know without seeing the horse whether he is lazy by nature, as some are, or whether he is lazy due to lack of knowledge or acceptance of the aids. If it is the former, it will be difficult to change his character, so maybe you will need to use him for something which he enjoys, i.e. jumping, hunting, hacking, etc. If it is the latter, which can probably only be ascertained by someone with experience of different types of horses, you will need to work on making him go forward from the leg aids. The help of a schooling whip and possibly spurs may have to come into it, as he will need to learn to respect the leg and answer a squeeze, which he will not do from constant kicking by the rider.

If he should kick out, buck or nap to the stick, careful and firmer use of the whip will have to be employed. Sometimes this can be distressing to the rider, but seldom to the horse, as they have very thick skins!

Determination from the rider will ultimately triumph over stubbornness by the horse, which seems only reasonable, since we have them for our pleasure!

Feeding and work can play a part in making horses more willing, as a fit horse will be able to work better and harder than one which is filled up with bulk, instead of suitable short feeds, or worked inconsistently.

Question: I have been told that I should 'ride my horse in' each day before starting work. Could you explain what this means and how long it should last?

Answer: 'Riding in' is a term used meaning loosening up the horse and preparing him for the harder work to follow. If he has come straight from the stable he may be a little stiff and his muscles will need time to warm up, and become elastic. The length of time for 'riding in' will depend upon how quickly this happens, and of course each horse will vary in this respect.

The time could be divided as follows:

Begin with walk on a long rein round the school with changes of direction.

I personally do not agree with a loose rein as I think that the horse should accept a contact from the start, although he will be allowed to stretch, and go forwards and down to the bit.

Then, similarly, in rising trot, to allow the back to come free and round. Include some large circles.

Continue with canter in the same way.

Finish the 'riding in' with a walk on a free rein to allow complete relaxation mentally and physically before the commencement of the lesson.

Question: Do I do the same exercises every day?

Answer: In order to establish a new exercise in the horse's mind, repetition is important. Whatever is worked upon one day needs a follow-up the day after, and probably for several consecutive days. Once it is clear and the horse willingly and easily gives to the aids of that exercise, it may be repeated at greater intervals. The exercises which the horse already knows will probably be part of the general routine, and will be used towards the build-up of the training.

However, although suppling, straightening and overall work on aids acceptance is necessary each day, I do not believe that the horse should necessarily be made to work through everything he knows every day. There is usually some particular thing one wants to improve. Exercises should be used to this end, and when sufficient improvement on that point is made, the lesson may end for that day.

Question: If I am having a problem with an exercise, should I carry on until I get it perfect?

Answer: Bearing in mind the supreme difficulty in obtaining perfection, it is probably wiser to accept only improvements. Sometimes one has to settle for very small ones and be satisfied. With any problem it may be important to struggle for a while in order to make progress. It would be helpful to assess whether the problem is caused by naughtiness or confusion.

4

If it is naughtiness then one should pursue the matter until the horse will accept what he is being asked and some distinct improvement is attained.

If it is confusion, then the horse will be upset and tense. It is not easy to be receptive in this condition so it may be as well to 'back off', to a degree, or even to change the exercise, temporarily. Then give time to reconsider your approach. Mostly, quiet perseverance overcomes the problem and will get you some way towards the ultimate goal.

Question: How many days a week shall I school?

Answer: It depends on each individual horse, his temperament and attitude. I think every horse deserves one day off per week!

Some feel quite neglected if they do not work six days a week, as they actually enjoy working. The ones who find it rather heavy going are best schooled every other day. Alternatively, three days running and then a hack or some other activity. I think when teaching a new exercise, the continuity is important, so you may need to work for several consecutive days and then have a break.

With a young horse allowance should be made for limited physical capacity for some time. He can learn new things quickly, but will need time to develop his muscles. Trained horses do not need the repetition daily unless they are competing a lot, when it will be important to keep them supple and obedient to detail.

Each rider must get to know his horse and train according to its energies.

Question: How long should I school for each day?

Answer: No-one can say exactly, as each horse is so different, and a lot depends on whether everything is going well, or whether one is struggling with a problem!

However, as a rough guide, I would say about an hour, but a quarter of an hour or so is 'loosening' the horse, and ten minutes or so at the end is 'cooling off', so the lesson would be half an hour or a little more. Some days it may well be less, if a particular lesson has been achieved well in a short time.

There is no point in keeping to a set time for the sake of it, as the important point is to teach the horse what he has to do. If he grasps it quickly, take him back to the stable or go for a hack. He will remember the exercise best in this way.

You do not have to go through an entire routine every day, when the horse is learning.

Question: How do I finish my schooling session each day?

Answer: I think there are two points involved.

First of all, it is important to the horse to finish on a good note, whatever length of time one has been schooling. Try to end with something you especially want the horse to remember the next time.

Secondly, the horse will need to cool off physically, and relax mentally, so a short period of time should be spent, in a free forward rising trot, allowing the horse to stretch, and then a free walk on a long rein. After which, he should be brought to a correct square halt on the aids, before the dismounting.

Question: I am told that my horse has wolf teeth. Is this why he tosses his head a lot?

Answer: Tossing heads are rarely caused by wolf teeth, but are much more likely to be due to poor co-ordination of the rider's hands and legs, and lack of discipline to the aids. Occasionally wolf teeth may interfere with the position of the

6

bit, so if your horse has them, it may be worth getting the vet to check on this for you.

I know vets who say that they mostly remove wolf teeth, to please the owner, not because they really are going to make any difference. Sharp teeth are probably more likely to cause trouble, so it is wise to have the horse's mouth checked at least once a year.

Question: I can't carry a stick as my horse is terrified of them. Shall I use spurs?

Answer: I have come across this problem many times, and so far, I have not found a horse which will not accept a schooling whip eventually, if properly used.

The problem is presumably caused by the horse having had a beating for something, either in the stable or ridden, for some specific reason. Sometimes it is not possible to carry a whip to start with, if the horse is very nervous. Give him time to get to know you, and realise that you are not going to hurt him. Once he begins to gain confidence, take a short whip and carry it on one side only. After a few days, change it to the other hand.

Once this is achieved, try changing it from one hand to the other, very quietly, in halt. After a day or two try this in walk, and so on.

It will depend on the horse's reaction as to how long you will need to do this before trying the whole procedure again with a schooling whip. Try to choose a fairly stiff one, as anything that flaps at the end could cause a problem. They tend to flick the horse when you don't want them to.

When the horse is calm with you carrying the whip, the next step is to teach him to allow you to use it, to aid the leg. This should be approached by degrees. First, in halt just rest the whip on the horse's flank just behind the leg, and soothe him with the voice. Then stroke him gently with the end of it still behind the leg. He will soon accept this when he realises nothing terrible is going to happen. After a few days, try a

7

gentle tap. He will probably jump forwards, but of course that is the reaction you want so long as it is not followed by panic.

It may take some months before it is possible to use the whip as it should be used, which is to make the horse more responsive, and therefore lighter to the leg aids. During this time the horse will become more trained anyway and therefore more obedient.

With the greater control, the introduction of the whip will become easier in any case. I do not believe that without the aid of a schooling whip one can satisfactorily train a horse, its help is required in many ways. Therefore I think it important to teach the horse to accept it.

I do not find that spurs are a substitute so I would not use them instead.

Question: I have noticed a lot of dressage riders wearing spurs. Should I wear them and, if so, when do I start?

Answer: Much depends on the type of horse you have and the reason for wearing them. The reason for doing so is probably the most important point.

Spurs are not actually required to be worn in dressage competitions, until Medium standard, but should be introduced at home before that to allow the horse to become accustomed to them. They should not be worn in order to coerce the horse to go forward, but are intended to enable the rider to use a finer aid.

Therefore, prodding and poking at the horse's sides is incorrect and frequently dulls the leg aid instead of making it more effective. It may make the horse very resentful and even nappy. Many riders do use spurs instead of making their horse answer a light leg aid by reinforcing it with the schooling whip.

Some very lazy horses may need a spur as well as the leg and whip but, if that is their nature, they are not very suitable for dressage. Excitable horses will take longer to accept the feel of a spur, and will only do so when totally accepting the rider's leg aids.

Question: As my horse is young and untrained should I rise or sit when I am schooling in trot?

Answer: In principle, it is probably better for a young horse's back, mostly, to rise. This leaves the muscles free and allows him the chance to 'round', rather than hollow his back. This is important as it prevents tension, which if it occurs, causes stiffness and eventually resistance. Most riders will rise anyway at the 'warming up' stage of a schooling session to allow the horse to 'free' himself.

Experts with good established positions may decide to 'sit', quite a bit, subsequently. If the seat is less secure, damage can be done to the horse's back by bumping about inadvertently.

Question: My horse carries his head too high. Is it alright to use running (draw) reins to get it down?

Answer: There are times when it may be necessary to employ the assistance of a running rein temporarily, either because the conventional method simply won't work, or for some particular exercise. This is normally only necessary if the horse's mouth is thoroughly spoiled, or he has developed a very strong muscle under his neck from having been allowed to go 'above the bit', or if he is a very big, tough horse who uses his strength continually against the rider.

I do think it is preferable to try to achieve submission by using the legs and hands and teaching the horse to soften his mouth by patience and using suppling exercises, i.e. flexions, shoulder-in, etc.

Question: I usually jump my horse in a martingale. Should I take it off to school him?

Answer: I think you should try. Any additional piece of equipment used reduces the true effect of the legs and hands, with which we really want to achieve a result. Temporary use of gadgets can be very helpful if all else has failed. Also it depends how they are fitted.

Standing martingales have no training value at all. Running martingales can sometimes be of assistance with an older horse, if it has learned to get very much above the bit. However, if they are too tight they will tend to drag the head down into an overbent position as the hind legs are driven up. Also there is a danger that riders will use it only to get the head down *without* driving the hind legs up. Usually in this case the horse will revert to the 'above bit' position when the martingale is removed.

Question: When should I put my horse into a double bridle?

Answer: It depends what you want to do.

Many riders want to 'show' as well as do dressage, and the 'dress' for the class may require a double bridle. In this case it may have to be introduced earlier than the rider doing 'pure' dressage. Either way, I believe that the horse should be quite happy, accepting the aids in the various gaits and transitions, and be knowledgeable about bend before any other bit is introduced. Then he may be ridden in the double, either in the school, or out hacking, but with more accent on the bradoon.

There is a misconception often regarding the curb chain. A loose curb chain is not doing the horse a kindness as it allows far too much leverage of the arm of the bit. A tighter chain will be rather like having 'air brakes', but if used carefully will enable the rider to use more refined aids.

A double bridle is not required in dressage competitions

till Advanced standard, although it may be used from Elementary upwards.

Horses should be able to do all the Grand Prix movements in a snaffle, but are required to do the tests in a double.

The double bridle is used for containing the gradually increasing impulsion and collection, so until you are reaching this stage there is no particular point in introducing it.

Question: Should my horse be on the bit out hacking?

Answer: I think that the important point to remember is that if the horse is to become trained, the aids must be consistent. Also the rider should realise that the horse can either be on the bit, or on a loose rein, and that there is nothing in between!

It is possible to ride on a long rein on the bit or on a short rein on the bit, but any inconsistent contact will result in a hard mouth and unsteady head.

Therefore, I would say in answer to the question, that if one is to enjoy a hack (which most people do for relaxation) but to still be safe, it is best to do part of the ride 'on the bit' on a short rein, and the remainder on a long rein 'on the bit'.

I would like to draw attention to the fact that trotting or cantering, especially in the company of others, can be dangerous unless the horse is controlled. He can only be truly controlled if he is 'on the bit'!

Question: Should my horse have a holiday, and for how long?

Answer: No doubt opinions vary about holidays.

I believe that a long period allows the dressage horse to become too slack and lose his muscle tone. This can cause difficulties in maintaining the required suppleness.

Mentally, the horse may need a break from concentrated

learning and it may be better to give short breaks more frequently. For example, early spring, mid-summer and autumn, for no more than one week at a time.

He can be turned out for a few hours each day to rest, but not 'turned away', as an eventer would be. If the horse is 'turned away', owners must be prepared to bring the horse up slowly in order to get him fit again, and to bring muscles back to full working order.

Question: Is it possible for any horse to learn dressage, or do you have to have a particular type?

Answer: The answer to this is that you can certainly train any horse to do dressage, but some will have a limit which they reach, which may fall far short of Grand Prix.

There will be those which can be trained up to Grand Prix level but due to conformation difficulties, or lack of stride, will never be brilliant.

The horses which are most likely to do well should start with good conformation, a naturally good stride and temperament. Those horses which are exceedingly idle or very nervous will be unlikely to progress far. A horse with very upright shoulders will probably not have much freedom of movement. Others which are long in the back will have more difficulty in engaging their hindquarters, as will those who are 'high behind'.

Most horses can achieve most dressage movements, but riders should be aware of their shortcomings and limitations, only expecting brilliance from a really talented horse.

Question: My horse takes very short steps in walk, is there anything I can do?

Answer: It depends upon what sort of walk your horse does naturally when he is loose in the field. Some horses unfortunately are not blessed with a long walk stride so with the best will in the world there is very little that can be done.

However, some horses do 'shorten up' when ridden. They may do this because they are restricted by their rider, probably the most common reason, or they may get shorter because they are hurrying too much and overbalancing.

I think the first thing to do, having established that the stride is naturally long, is to walk on a long rein. Allow the horse complete freedom to take his maximum length stride. If he hurries, restrain him, and then give the rein, until he will walk slowly, without contact. Gradually then begin to make contact, ensuring that you do not restrict the horse at all. If he remains calm it should gradually be possible to use the legs to squeeze him forwards to the contact, which can then begin to bring him onto the bit.

It will be a help to the horse's relaxation if you relax your own seat muscles and allow yourself and the horse to swing along together. Any tension from you will make him tighten his back muscles which will probably result in shortening of the steps.

Question: What can I do to make my horse lengthen his neck in the free walk?

Answer: I know that this problem does cause many people a lot of heartache! I do believe however that if, or when, the horse works correctly from behind through his back, and accepts the bit, he will want to lower when given a free rein. In the meantime you can assist the process by first, making him relaxed when he comes to walk. Avoid any hurrying or tension in yourself. Try squeezing him forward by using your legs asking him to soften in the mouth, using an alternate feel and ease contact on each side. Then offer a lighter rein contact to see whether he will go down. He may go 'a little', in which case repeat the process on the longer rein and try the 'offering' again, and again until he reaches the stretching you are looking for.

It may take some time but this 'working down' should succeed if you are patient.

The free walk on a long rein should entail keeping a very light contact. If this is done it will be possible to remind the horse that he can stay stretched, using the above method, until it is time to bring him together.

Question: I am told that my collected walk is irregular. What can I do about it?

Answer: Difficulties often occur when collection is required. This is due to a discrepancy in the true acceptance of the aids, either by legs or hands or both.

This discrepancy manifests itself in resistance in the mouth, poll or back of the horse. Any resistance causes muscle 'blockage' which can result in uneven steps. This can be in front or behind, one foot taking a shorter stride than the other. This would be described as irregular.

There are at least two other possibilities. Some horses will show resistance to collection by lifting their front feet higher than their back feet, giving an appearance of the Spanish Walk. This can be overcome by making them go more forwards and achieving better acceptance of the bit.

An even more unpleasant resistance, in my opinion, is an untrue walk sequence, which is more readily understood, as 'pacing', where the feet on the same side come forward together instead of separately. It can be quite difficult to correct but is generally associated with too much speed and tension.

Half-halts to reduce speed and a calming influence by the rider should aid relaxation and bring about a truer walk.

Question: In extended walk I am uncertain how much rein to give. Can you help?

Answer: In the extended walk the horse should walk out to

his maximum ability, his back feet overtracking the print which the forefoot leaves.

In order to achieve this he needs to stretch his head and neck forward, the nose being slightly in front of the vertical. He can only do this if he is allowed to have his neck lower than he would for medium, or collected walk, but not lower than a horizontal line from the withers. You should give sufficient rein to allow all this to happen, whilst maintaining a light contact with the horse's mouth.

Normally a stretching forward of the rider's arm will give the leeway required, and make it unnecessary to actually lengthen the reins.

Question: In the walk pirouette my horse's hind legs always seem to get stuck so that he swivels round. Could you give me advice on how to correct this?

Answer: The first thing to do is to decide what the walk is like coming into the half pirouette. It needs to be very active and collected so that the steps are shortened and heightened.

The next thing to do is to make your pirouette bigger. If the hind legs are swivelling, the walk has actually stopped, so think of keeping up the impulsion and then try to make the hind legs make a small half circle.

It may help to think of doing a half pass with the quarters in so that the whole horse comes round the pirouette, curved in the direction in which he is going, stepping forwards and coming round at the same time.

When you have mobility of the hind feet, try reducing the size of the pirouette until you get it marking time behind. If it goes wrong again, go forwards and try again.

Do remember the importance of using the inside leg to keep up the impulsion, but beware also of muddling the horse by pushing him away from it, as this would totally contradict the outside leg which is preventing the quarters from swinging out.

Question: My horse's trot has been described as 'flat'. What does this mean and is there anything I can do?

Answer: Horses can vary a lot in the quality of their trot and in the amount of spring they have in their stride.

If you can visualise the way the legs move in trot you can probably appreciate how the trot could be described as 'flat'. The legs move diagonally, each pair coming to the ground alternately: i.e. near fore, off hind; off fore, near hind.

As each pair leaves the ground there should be a moment of suspension. Some horses will, naturally, show this clearly and others less so. If the horse does not naturally have this moment of suspension, the rider has to endeavour to create one.

Developing a good regular stride in a steady rhythm helps to produce this, but it is not possible without energy (impulsion) and activity of the hind legs, coming under the horse enabling him to 'lift' himself.

Some trots can be difficult to improve but most will do so by gradual building up of impulsion and collection.

Question: I have always understood that a horse should have good suspension in trot which my horse naturally has, but I seem to be losing marks constantly in competition for being too elevated. Is this so wrong?

Answer: You are certainly correct in that a horse should show a moment of suspension between one diagonal and the other. You are fortunate if your horse has this naturally.

Unfortunately, as with everything, there are things which can go wrong. I expect what is happening is that your horse is not going forward with sufficient energy. He may be using his natural elevation as an evasion to working really hard enough. His elevation must be combined with impulsion to take him forwards, not simply upwards.

When you trot your horse try to assess whether he is 'covering ground', getting where he is going energetically, or whether the whole thing feels 'slow motion'. Too much elevation at a slow speed will be too much like a low passage, and would certainly lose marks.

For a time you may have to try to increase the tempo to get him out of this habit. Riding forwards more energetically will gradually achieve this.

When you get to collection you may come up against the same problem again, but using variation within the gait (i.e. lengthening and shortening the stride) and transitions, with firm seat and leg to keep him forward to the hand, will help.

Question: I am told that I should have my horse regular in trot. I am not really sure what this means?

Answer: The word regular is used to describe steps which are rhythmic.

In dressage competitions one of the main requirements is that a horse should show good regular (rhythmic) gaits. It is only possible to achieve regularity, if the speed (tempo) of the steps is steady. If there is rushing, due to tension, lack of balance, etc. the speed will vary and the rhythm (regularity) with it.

One of the first things to do in training is to establish a speed at which the horse can work in balance, so that a rhythm can develop. Obviously a good deal depends on the rider's feel and ability to keep his horse's gaits regular.

Question: When do I start teaching my horse to do lengthened trot?

Answer: I think that there may be some variance of opinion as to whether the stride should be lengthened before or after teaching the horse some collection. It also may depend on the horse's stride.

However, there are several factors which are important in any case.

First, the balance of the horse in trot should be established sufficiently that if any change in the gait is asked for he does not immediately tip onto the forehand.

Secondly, it is important that the horse should be straight and therefore very even in the stride. Any crookedness will cause unlevel steps which is not only incorrect, but will also make it more difficult for the horse to comply with the rider's aids.

Thirdly, the horse will not easily lengthen his trot if he is insufficiently 'on the aids'.

Finally, unless the hind legs are working under the horse, he will be unable to lengthen satisfactorily.

I believe, therefore, that an element of collection resulting from the use of the half-halt to bring the horse together, is really necessary before attempting lengthening.

Question: I am not clear how I should achieve extensions in the various paces. How is this achieved?

Answer: All extensions rely on a build up of energy and balance. This build up is based on the ability to make a variation within the gait, in a small way at first, using half-halts, the horse responding instantly to being brought together, or sent forwards.

When this small variation is achieved smoothly, without resistance, and maintaining a regular rhythmic stride, the horse is prepared for a greater lengthening of the same.

Greater controlled impulsion plus the ability to collect, will gradually enable the horse to produce a longer stride in the same rhythm, without losing balance. If the horse falls onto his forehand he will be unable to produce a longer stride. Similarly, if he fails to respond to the leg aids, or leans against the hand, he will not be in a position to respond sufficiently.

Question: Whenever I try to ride a serpentine in trot my horse puts his head up in the middle of it and is marked down in competitions. Can you tell me why he does this?

Answer: Generally speaking, horses alter the position of their head and neck to save their balance.

In this case I would guess that your horse is more stiff on one side than the other and is failing to give an equal bend in each direction. To make it easier for himself he alters his head position. I think you should go back to circles for a time and make sure that he answers your inside leg.

Also, the shoulder-in exercise is invaluable for gaining better control of bend.

Question: When I am cantering, every time I want to circle, and quite often in the corners, he changes legs behind and becomes disunited. How can I prevent this happening?

Answer: The reason your horse changes legs behind is partly lack of balance, but mostly, stiffness. He is resisting the bend you require for the start of a circle or coming into a corner.

You can help him by making him more supple in walk and trot, really making him bend round your inside leg, using circles of varying sizes, and the shoulder-in exercise. This should also help to improve his ability to answer your aids in the canter as well, and make him more balanced. Do make sure that he is listening to both leg aids, the inside one sending him forward, and the outside keeping the quarters round the inside leg.

When you come to canter again the situation should be better, but if it is still not satisfactory, use your outside leg and outside rein together. This temporarily removes the bend, but he will not be able to change legs behind if there is sufficient control from the outside hand.

Gradually you will be able to re-take the bend.

Question: When I give my aids for canter or if I want to go more forwards in canter, my horse sometimes humps his back. What is he doing and why?

Answer: First of all check that there is nothing wrong with your horse's back. Make sure that the saddle is not rubbing him and making him sore, and that it is not pinching him. If all is well then the answer is that the horse is resisting the leg aids. A form of 'napping'.

He has discovered that if he humps his back, he can push your seat out of the saddle. This reduces its effectiveness, allowing him to do his 'own thing', and work far less hard than he should. For a time he will probably need the use of the schooling whip to reinforce the leg aids. If he gets a sharp smack he will realise that his little game is not on!

Send him forwards strongly from seat and leg every time he humps so that you have more impulsion. When you control this energy make sure that you keep him well forwards to the hand, and do not let him drop behind the leg, or come off the bit.

Use plenty of variations within the gait and be determined!

Question: My horse won't strike off on the left leg in canter. What do I do?

Answer: Persistent difficulty in obtaining the correct lead in canter can be particularly tiresome for the novice rider.

Experience generally overcomes this problem quite quickly as the horse usually strikes off correctly if put in the right position.

Less knowledgeable riders find it difficult to feel this positioning. There are several ways to try to overcome the problem.

A horse will 'strike off' more readily on the inside lead if he is asked for it in a corner of the school, or on a circle. Try to achieve a fairly active trot initially with the horse going

20

forwards well into the bridle. He should be as balanced as possible.

If he will not answer the correct aids: i.e. inside leg on the girth, outside leg behind the girth, inside rein asking a very small flexion, outside rein controlling the speed and size of the circle or corner, then the use of the schooling whip behind the outside leg should be employed. A sharp tap with the schooling whip and a strong aid from the inside leg should make the 'strike off'.

However, if the horse has seldom cantered on the correct leg, either because he is stubborn, or because he has never been made to do so, it may be necessary to make him take 'outside bend' into the strike off.

In other words, the rider will take a strong flexion to the outside of the circle or corner, away from the leg upon which he wants the horse to lead. This will have the effect of putting extra weight onto the outside shoulder, freeing the inside leg. To save his balance the horse may strike off correctly.

If the correct lead is obtained it is important to keep the canter going, for one or two circuits of the school or field, to give the horse the idea that he can canter on that leg.

Another horse positioned in the centre of the circle may encourage some horses to strike off correctly. In extreme cases a pole or cavaletti placed on the track in a corner of the school will sometimes do the trick. Trot the horse over it and push on as you get there. The horse will probably partly jump which will cause him to canter and I have found that in most cases he will land on the inside lead.

It is important to recognise when the correct lead is achieved, and if the rider fails to push on quickly, the horse may fall back to trot and will not learn what he is meant to do.

Question: How can I stop my horse putting its head up going into canter?

Answer: This is a very common difficulty and often tiresome to correct.

Theoretically, the answer is to make the horse more obedient to the aids. Practically, it can be hard to achieve. I believe that the horse does this to help 'lift' himself into canter, but if this is necessary it does indicate insufficient energy driving him into that gait.

I have found that increasing energy in the trot and containing it in the hand, certainly helps. This, with an increased action of the squeezing of the fingers prevents the mouth 'setting' in the moment of 'strike off'. If the horse (and rider) understands a shoulder-in 'position', this is very helpful in overcoming this problem.

Shoulder-in at walk or in trot should be taken on the long side. Coming into a corner reduce the angle, but keep the aids on and then ask at once for the canter. This is also very useful for horses who are difficult about a certain leg.

Question: I constantly have trouble in canter with my horse carrying his 'quarters in'. I have tried to push them out but it seems to make matters worse. What can I do?

Answer: Any attempt at pushing out quarters which are carried in from the track will certainly be ineffective. The correction should be made to the forehand by taking a 'shoulder-in' position. It may be necessary to first effect some straightening of the horse's neck, as almost certainly, it will be curled inwards as well. This should be done by using more outside rein into the neck, not only to straighten the neck, but to prevent too much weight being carried on the outside shoulder.

If the shoulder-in can be performed satisfactorily in trot, the horse will know the aids, and it should be possible to use these aids to obtain a shoulder-in position in canter.

Once the forehand has been positioned, the quarters will sort themselves out and begin to follow the forehand correctly.

Question: I am trying to teach my horse counter canter, but find that he keeps changing legs in front. What can I do to prevent this?

Answer: Your horse is changing legs and becoming disunited because he is lacking in balance.

Try riding a very shallow loop on the side of the school, with only a small gradual deviation from the track. Make sure you start the loop at the first quarter marker after the short side, come off the track a little, run parallel to it for a few strides and then gradually take him back to the track at the quarter marker at the end of the long side.

Although the flexion should be maintained to the leading leg, avoid too much bend until the horse has learned the exercise. Keep him as equal to both hands and legs as you can, but try to give more support to the shoulder opposite to the leading leg by keeping that rein well in to the neck.

Your outside leg should be a little further back than usual to keep him to the leading leg. You will need more push during your loop to keep the impulsion.

Do also make sure that you have a steady enough canter to be able to ask for counter lead as if there is too much speed the horse will lose his balance and change legs whatever you do.

Question: In my canter pirouette I find that I lose control and the horse seems to get round quicker than I do! What is wrong?

Answer: Your horse is being over helpful! He obviously knows the exercise and as soon as he feels you tell him to start, decides to get it over as quickly as possible. There must be a certain amount of tension, I imagine, for this to arise as speed often is connected to anxiety. You should check up on two points to begin with. First, make sure that the horse is calm in his canter and is rounded in his outline. Also, that he will let you 'position' him in canter. That is to say, a very small shoulder-in position. He must do this without getting steamed up.

Question: I have been trying to teach my horse to do canter pirouettes but he lifts very high in front and seems to be in 'slow motion'. Can you suggest what I might do?

Answer: The most important factor in the canter pirouette is to actually keep the canter! This is not meant to be a facetious remark. It is the difficult part of the exercise.

If the canter is true and short (collected) enough, the coming round is no problem. If your horse is tending to lift his forehand to get round, basically he has lack of impulsion. He is trying to comply with the aids, labouring in the process, his hind legs getting stuck to the spot as he heaves his forehand round.

I would suggest a re-think on your collected canter. Is it really collected enough and does the horse stay 'round' in his outline? Can he do an almost 'on the spot' canter for a few strides at a time in the same tempo? If the tempo is slowing then he needs more leg from the rider creating energy to keep the activity.

I suggest that you ride the pirouette more forward and make it bigger until you can come round in a true canter, keeping him rounded with the correct tempo and bend.

Question: My canter pirouette is sometimes described by dressage judges as a 'turn on the centre'. Can you explain exactly what this means and what I should do?

Answer: In a canter pirouette the hind feet describe a very small circle almost on the spot, and the forehand makes a bigger circle. This is achieved by the rider controlling the hindquarters with the inside leg on the girth to keep the canter, and the outside leg behind the girth to prevent the quarters swinging out. The hands are bringing the forehand round by the use of the inside rein to flex the horse in the direction he is going, and the outside rein controlling speed, collection and the size of the stride as it comes round.

In a full pirouette approximately eight strides would complete the exercise. Because it is hard work, very often the horse may evade the proper use of the pirouette, in which, the horse must lower the hindquarters and bring the hind legs further under his body to support his forehand. He will evade in various ways but one way is to try to swing his quarters out against the rider's outside leg. In this way he will avoid 'sitting', where he would have to flex his joints more, and gets away with a stiff back and an incorrect exercise.

In this case the forehand may eventually come round to the new direction, but the quarters will not have described a smaller circle. This is often called turn on the centre.

A good exercise for correcting this evasion is to canter a small circle. Start with a 10m (33ft) circle and position the quarters in. When the horse is attending better to the rider's outside leg, the size of the circle can gradually be reduced until a pirouette is achieved.

At all times it should be possible to bring the horse back onto a true circle if desired.

In the build up to the full pirouette, alternate quarters in, the true circle should give greater control, giving the rider a chance to feel what is happening, and the horse time to balance.

Question: In the canter half pass I find it very difficult to get any bend. Could you advise me?

Answer: There are several factors to consider.

First of all, think about the sort of canter you have. Is it collected enough? Does it have enough impulsion? It will be very difficult for your horse to give the bend you need if he is strung out or lacking in energy.

Also, can you ride a circle of 8 or 10m (26 or 33ft) with a

good bend? This is the sort of curve that the horse will need to make in the half pass. You will have to be able to make him curve round your inside leg from the use of your outside leg and be able to take a shoulder-in position with the forehand.

He will need to be very responsive to your inside leg, as it is this leg which will be responsible for maintaining, or increasing if necessary, the energy and the bend. It is this leg too, which must also maintain the 'lift' of the canter as, if this is lost, the horse will not be able to gain ground in the moment of suspension. Additionally, the inside leg must prevent the horse falling onto his inside shoulder which will certainly cause loss of bend. Its correct use will keep the canter upright and forward to the hand enabling the rider to shape the bend of the forehand.

Question: How do I correct 'swinging' flying changes?

Answer: Whenever there is a crookedness in training, the solution is to ride the horse more forward.

'Swinging' changes are generally caused by a crookedness in the canter. This is most likely to be on the side to which the horse prefers to hollow himself. Most horses try to do this, but more expert riders will prevent it happening.

For example, on the right rein the horse will bend his neck too much to the inside and try also to carry his quarters to the right. In the flying change from the left to the right he will adopt this quarters-in position as he changes, which will cause a swing. He may also try to jump to the right, making it impossible to keep a straight line. As with any crookedness in the canter the correction is made to the forehand, not the quarters directly.

If a shoulder-in position is taken, together with a stronger inside leg to send the horse more forward, a straightening is effected. This method is carried through the 'changes', and although resistances may be encountered to start with, the horse will gradually allow himself to be made straighter and more controlled.

Question: My horse keeps being 'late behind' in his flying changes. What can I do about this?

Answer: I think that this fault, like most faults in the flying change, depends very much on the quality of the canter itself.

Basically, the canter must be going forwards with plenty of impulsion so that there is a good moment of suspension. This is important because that moment of suspension is when the flying change occurs, so if it is too flat, there will be no room for the change to be made.

The impulsion will also be important in order to collect the horse and ensure that he is not on his forehand. Late changes often occur because there is too much weight on the horse's shoulders. This gives the quarters too much opportunity to become high, enabling the horse to make short or late changes with a hind leg.

As with all exercises, the better the horse accepts the aids, the better the chance of correct changes. The rider must be very clear with his aids and well co-ordinated.

The rider's inside leg will be of particular importance in obtaining the flying change, as its positive use will send the horse forward and obtain the new bend. The effective action of this inside leg will certainly help to reduce the chance of late changes.

Late changes do also happen very often because the rider has either failed to change the bend as the aid is given with the legs, or because the horse resists the change of bend and falls onto his inside shoulder. If this is happening, try changing the flexion a little before the leg aids so that the horse is more prepared and partly already in position.

Question: How do I teach my horse to stand square?

Answer: Some horses naturally bring themselves to a square halt, and others persistently do not. Whatever happens, it is acceptance of the aids coming into halt that helps in the first place.

In the early stages with novice or young horses, it may be wise to accept a 'straight' halt, even if it is not quite square. If the horse is calm, correction may be attempted by the rider using the legs to bring the horse more together. If this does not work, a schooling whip may be used very lightly on the offending leg.

Praise must be given for a correct response. An assistant on the ground could use a whip lightly on any leg left behind, to aid the rider.

Also, as a matter of discipline, always try to make your horse stand square for mounting, grooming and on the lunge. It will then become a matter of habit and be easier to achieve when ridden.

Question: My horse won't stand still. How do I make him?

Answer: Horses vary in the ways in which they won't stand still. Some are merely ignorant and not very bright, and wander or move about at will, unless the rider is really firm.

Young horses will lack an understanding as to what is being required of them. Nervous horses can be worried at being made to stand as they tend to feel 'dropped' by the aids. Some may be anxious because they have been made to 'square up', and keep moving a foot hoping that this is what is wanted. Whatever the reason, better use of aids should help.

When your horse really accepts the legs and the bit, he can be brought to a halt under control. A pat or praising by the voice should soothe the anxious horse, and in time will penetrate the brain of the 'thick' horse, that to 'stand still' is what is required. Do be careful not to 'hang on' to the horse's mouth in halt as this will make him want to evade the hands. It is also a mistake to take the legs away as then there is

28

nothing to hold the horse forward to the hands, or to control the quarters.

Calmness is essential in achieving a good halt. Firm aids and repetition should help.

Question: How and when do I start teaching collection?

Answer: The horse should be going well forwards from the legs and be submissive to the bit. He should be straight, balanced and holding a steady regular stride. He should be able to do half-halts.

He would then be sufficiently prepared to learn some shortened steps, which are achieved from the use of the half-halt. They may be sustained for a few strides in order that the horse learns to re-balance. He will try to vary the impulsion but it should be kept forward to the hand, aided by the schooling whip, if necessary. He may come heavy in the hand to begin with, but as he finds his balance should be able to lighten.

The rider must keep the horse straight and ride energetically but smoothly forward after the shortening. This process is repeated over a period of days or weeks until the horse can hold the shorter strides for himself.

Gradually then, more impulsion is asked for so that the horse may become more compressed, and then ask him to sustain the collection over longer periods.

Question: How do I know if I have got my horse collected?

Answer: There is quite a positive difference when you have got it right.

The hindquarters feel more under the horse's body, and are full of energy. The steps feel more springy and 'off the ground'. The back feels spongelike to sit on. The forehand

29

feels higher, the neck arching up in front. The head feels more bent at the poll, the nose further in towards a vertical position, with the mouth 'giving' to the hands. The movements all seem easier to ride.

It is possible to be misled, by the steps being shorter but not higher, due to lack of impulsion. Also the horse may feel compressed, but only because he has drawn back in his neck but has not brought up his quarters.

He may be shortening, but be hollow in the back instead of round, which will give the feel of sitting in a dish. The back will probably be hard instead of soft.

In collection the hind feet should not come into the print which the forefoot leaves, as the impulsion gives more elevation to the steps.

Question: Can you explain the difference between impulsion and activity, or are they the same thing?

Answer: I think that impulsion means to most people, the energy in the hindquarters which takes the horse forward. Activity is the effort which the hind legs make in respect of flexion of the joints, which give 'lift' to the stride.

Some horses one sees are very active behind but do not go forwards as well, and some are driving themselves along but with very little flexion of the joints.

Question: I am always being told I should use more half-halts in training, but I don't think I really understand what they are. Could you enlighten me?

Answer: Half-halts are invaluable during training for many reasons. They, basically, help to balance the horse which, of course, is essential to correct work. They are used to steady excitable horses; to engage lazy horses, bring about collection, and for preparation for many exercises.

30

Before one can ride a half-halt, it is necessary to be able to ride correct transitions with the horse remaining 'on the aids'. He must allow himself to be ridden forward from the seat and leg into the bridle without resistance, accepting the bringing together of the hindquarters and the forehand. When this is performed with ease, then the half-halt or semi-transition may be introduced.

Think of it as almost a transition to the next gait, but not quite. A kind of 'pause', but without loss of impulsion. It is only momentary and it is very important that the horse goes forward immediately following. Bear in mind that the purpose of the half-halt is to balance or rebalance the horse, so in riding forward after it, do not then push him back onto his forehand or out of the rhythm.

Half-halts may be used in varying degrees. With a young or novice horse the degree will probably be smaller than with an older, more knowledgeable one.

Most half-halts fail because riders do not use the leg aids sufficiently so do bear this in mind.

Question: My horse will not bend to the left, what shall I do?

Answer: If your horse has difficulty in giving a bend to the left, it is probably because he has been allowed to keep his head to the right most of the time.

The muscles on the right-hand side of his neck will therefore be contracted, so when you try to take a left bend, the shortened muscles prevent him from giving one. Your first aim should be to get him straight and by riding him with more even contact from leg and hand. When he is straighter then ask for a small flexion to the left, and gradually, over a period of time, ask for more.

Circles and shoulder-in on both reins will help to make his muscles more even.

Question: My horse is on the forehand. How do I stop this happening?

Answer: The reason he is on the forehand is that his balance is incorrect. His weight should be carried more equally over his four legs, with a gradual transfer to the hindquarters, as training progresses.

The exercises which will help this transfer are transitions and half-halts. These need to be ridden properly, of course. Improvement will only be achieved by using the legs to make more energy from behind, which will then be controlled and contained by the hands.

Providing there is no resistance to these aids, the hind legs will come further under the body, improving distribution of weight, thus lightening the forehand.

Question: Does the turn on the forehand have any real use in training. If so, when would it be used?

Answer: I believe that the main purpose for teaching the horse this exercise is primarily to teach him to yield to the pressure of the rider's inside leg, for the purpose of being able to move the hindquarters away from any object, human or otherwise, which might be likely to cause danger, either to the object, or to the horse. It would normally be taught early in the young horse's training.

At one time it was thought that as the hindquarters moved round, the horse should be expected to pivot on his inside foreleg. However, nowadays this is not a criterion, the importance being laid upon the response the horse makes to the rider's leg aids.

Question: I do seem to have a lot of trouble keeping straight on a centre line. Can you help at all?

Answer: In walk and in trot it is only possible to keep straight if the horse is equally responsive to both legs and on both sides of his mouth. Also if he is equally supple.

In canter you should be able to take a 'shoulder-in' position to the leading leg in order to control the forehand. If the forehand is kept controlled, the quarters will be unable to wander and will follow the front.

In walk and trot, the rider should see the C marker between the horse's ears as he comes up the centre.

In canter and, indeed, at all times on the centre line, the rider must keep his eye on the C or A markers depending which way he is going, and immediately correct any slight deviation.

I think it is almost impossible to ride straight at any gait unless the horse knows the shoulder-in exercise, so that the forehand can be corrected. Any attempt to straighten the quarters without this control will only produce more swinging.

Question: I seem to be losing a lot of marks in transitions, because I am told my horse is 'not forward'. Could you explain what this means?

Answer: So often in transitions the rider uses the reins to slow the horse without sufficient support from the legs. This has the effect of stopping the impulsion, that energy which is taking the horse forward to the next gait. For a moment or even a few steps, that energy is lost or delayed which of course certainly affects the following movement, and probably allows the horse to fall on his forehand, lean on the hand, resist the bit and so on.

Although we are taught to use our legs, many riders are unaware of the extent to which this is necessary to keep the engagement of the hindquarters. In all transitions up and particularly down, firm use of a deep seat and strong legs will help to keep the horse forward and balanced.

Question: In circles I am continually losing marks in competitions for not having a 'true bend'. I do not understand what this means. Could you explain?

Answer: There could be several reasons why you are losing marks.

Horses which are stiff evade in quite a few ways. For instance, your horse could be tilting his head, crossing his jaw, leaning in, putting his hindquarters in, or escaping the bend by curling his neck round to the inside. This would also enable the outside shoulder to take too much weight allowing a 'drift' away from the true curve.

Try riding a few 20m (66ft) circles and assess which of these faults you have.

Whatever the fault is, the correct bend will only be improved by better acceptance to the aids.

In the case of tilting or crossing the jaw, it will be necessary to check up on the acceptance of the bit and see that the horse does so really equally.

If the neck is curling round too much, ride the horse straighter and make him listen to your inside leg, which also helps to prevent him leaning in. If the hindquarters are in, you will need to teach him shoulder-in to gain better control of his length. This will also correct any drifting away from the circle.

With circles of any size you must be clear in your mind and think of the shoulder-in aids.

Question: My horse puts his head up in rein back and goes rigid, refusing to go back. What can I do?

Answer: A horse can only rein back easily if his back is rounded, not hollow, and if he is correctly 'on the aids'.

If he is getting his head up he is escaping the aids, inevitably becoming hollow in his back, resulting in tense muscles which become painful if force is employed.

I think you should practise some transitions from walk to

halt to walk and so on until you are quite certain that you can keep him on the aids and in a rounded shape throughout those exercises. Do be sure to use your legs and keep them on the whole time including the pause of the halt.

When this seems satisfactory try the rein back from the halt using the legs, not too strongly, into a resisting hand. If the horse makes a step back remaining 'on the aids', pat him and walk on, repeating this and gradually increasing the number of steps back.

I think it important that the hand should ease between the steps to begin with, as slow deliberate steps are much more controllable and you do not want the horse to rush backwards.

If you still find you are having problems getting the horse to understand, try to get someone to help from the ground using a whip gently on the forelegs in turn, using your aids at the same time.

If you have taught the horse to step backwards using your voice in the stable, try this use of voice while mounted.

If he still tries to put his head up, ride forwards each time and correct him. I am sure patience will win through eventually.

Question: My horse's head always seems to be moving up and down. Why is this?

Answer: Unsteady head carriage is generally caused by the rider failing to keep a consistent or firm contact.

A firm contact can only be taken and maintained as the result of energy being created by the rider's legs, to make the horse go forwards into the bridle.

This energy is then controlled by the use of the reins. If the rider's contact is variable, the horse's mouth will receive intermittent messages, instead of a steady one. This will cause him to move his head, either fairly passively up and down, or possibly more violently, as he gets fed up with the discomfort in his mouth.

Question: When I ask my horse to come on the bit he puts his head in the air. What can I do?

Answer: The most important thing to do is to persevere and not be put off by the difficulty. Also, as with all aids, do have a think about the way you are asking him to come onto the bit.

He must first be answering the legs, listening to them in halt, and going forwards from them otherwise. Then he is asked to soften in the mouth by a squeezing action of the fingers probably used alternately, or held firmly on the softer side and squeezed at more firmly on the harder side.

Some horses can be very stubborn about yielding to the aids, but persistence on the part of the rider can overcome the problem.

Question: I am having trouble in keeping the angle in my shoulder-in. Can you help?

Answer: The answer rests in discovering whether you really have the horse accepting the inside leg and the outside rein, and whether the horse is sufficiently collected.

If he is truly answering the aids and is gathered together, it will be possible to control the angle.

Most mistakes occur due to the rider trying to take the angle from too much inside rein. This has the effect of bending the neck, rather than bringing the horse's shoulders off the track. A slack outside rein will allow the horse's shoulders to fall back into the track, and will make it impossible to keep the position. Failure to respond adequately to the rider's inside leg will cause loss of impulsion. This will prevent the horse's inside hind leg from coming up under his body, which he must do to be able to carry himself in a shoulder-in position.

The rider's outside leg must assist the exercise by controlling the hindquarters. If they swing out the horse's bend will be lost, in which case the exercise will end up as a leg yield, not a shoulder-in. Angle also may be changed if the collection is unsatisfactory.

If the horse is not well gathered together he will labour because he is too 'spread out', and be unable to do the exercise correctly.

Speed may also cause difficulties. If the steps are too quick and not keeping to a regular rhythm, the horse will run onto his outside shoulder thus losing his position.

Question: Do I need to teach my horse to do a leg yield before teaching it other lateral movements?

Answer: I think it can be quite an advantage to teach leg yielding with a novice horse, particularly for less experienced riders. It does give both the idea of going away from the leg.

More experienced riders will use a yield from the inside leg sometimes in corners or on a circle. It is not essential before teaching other lateral movements, if the rider has knowledge of those movements.

If it is taught, I believe the horse should be kept quite straight, so that there is no risk of the outside shoulder escaping.

Question: I always seem to lose the bend in a half pass. What am I doing wrong?

Answer: Successful half passes depend on several points.

The half pass cannot succeed unless there is sufficient impulsion coming forward to the hand. This impulsion must be created by the use of the rider's inside leg. There also has to be sufficient bend.

The bend is formed by the use of shoulder-in to put the shoulders in a position where they can take the horse forwards and across to where he is going. In order to be able to hold the bend and position, the horse will need to be collected.

The collection is achieved by use of half halts which keeps the stride short enough to enable the horse to move across laterally. The hindquarters will be required to come further round the rider's inside leg to make the bend, therefore the horse must be responsive to the outside leg aid.

If all these points are satisfactory, half pass should be possible.

However, there are a few additional points which might be helpful. Before even beginning to try a half pass, try riding a route from the centre line to the side line with a good flexion to the side you want the bend; i.e. in a 40 × 20 m (131 × 66 ft) area on right rein, turn up centre line. At D turn right towards M. Flex head, and neck a little, to right. Do not allow shoulders to deviate from that line.

Practise this several times on both reins.

Progress by coming up centre line and commencing two or three steps of shoulder-in (in canter shoulder-in position). Keeping the bend, position the shoulders towards the M marker and ride firmly forwards with the inside leg. If the bend is lost ride into shoulder-in again (in canter shoulder-in position), then try the half pass again.

Most mistakes are made by riders trying to push their horse across from the outside leg without putting the shoulders round towards the marker to which they are going. This causes dropping of impulsion and resistance because the angle is too difficult.

Riders often find the co-ordination of this exercise very difficult. Try thinking of bend aids for a circle. It is not quite that simple, but it may help.

In canter it is not possible to achieve the same shoulder-in angle as in trot, but a lesser degree of the exercise is possible. This is called shoulder-in position, rather than shoulder-in.

Question: I have taught my horse shoulder-in and half pass. Are there any other lateral movements which I should use?

38

Answer: There are two other lateral exercises related to the half pass, which are the Travers, or half pass head to wall, and Renvers (half pass tail to wall).

Both these movements would hold the same principles regarding aids, bend, collection, impulsion and so on, as the half pass, performed at an angle of 30 degrees to the wall or centre line.

There are also counter changes of hand, or zig zag, either in trot or canter.

Main points to look for are equal bend to each direction, correct number of steps, if specified, correct changes if performed in canter.

Question: In the counter changes of hand, I find that I continually get the quarters leading. Also, I can't seem to get in the number specified in the test I am trying to do. Can you help at all?

Answer: The correction to your problem regarding quarters leading in any of the lateral work is to correct the forehand.

If you take a slight shoulder-in position prior to your sideways movement, this will put the forehand a little ahead of the quarters. Then, if the horse bends round your inside leg, the angle of the lateral exercise will be correct.

Similarly during a counter change of hand, it will be necessary to put the forehand into shoulder-in position before asking the quarters to change direction.

Alternatively, it may help to finish one direction of the half pass and then take a Renvers position prior to the new direction. This also will put the shoulders into position, will keep the hindquarters under control and then all you have to do is to change the bend.

I expect that the reason you cannot get in the number of counter changes that you want is because the horse is lacking collection. You will need to work on improvement on this separately and before trying to fit in more changes of direction.

Question: I have been trying to teach my horse to piaffé but I am told he is doing passage steps. What does this mean and how can I stop him?

Answer: If this is happening, there could be two possible reasons:

First, he may be using steps which are too elevated to evade the difficulty of doing the exercise correctly.

Second, you may have impulsed him too much too soon before he really knows what is wanted.

Either way he must be got out of this quickly before it becomes too established, as it can become quite difficult to correct.

I do not know, of course, how you have been trying to teach your horse the piaffé. If you are teaching him mounted, as opposed to from the ground, you will need to make him more forward going to avoid the 'lifting' steps of the passage. To achieve this, try using transitions from trot to halt to trot, with only a brief pause for the halt.

When he is doing these transitions obediently with no resistances, try shortening the steps before and after the halt, but keeping the horse well in front of the leg. If he tries to drop the bit or hollow his back, ride forward energetically and then try again.

The steps out of the halt will gradually become shorter teaching the horse to lower his quarters, helping him to stay closer to the ground in the correct tempo.

Question: Could you tell me how to begin to teach passage?

Answer: If the piaffé and the transition from piaffé to trot is well under control, you may be ready to begin passage.

It will be important to have a very regular, collected trot, thout resistance, well forward and 'on the aids'. As the mpulsion is increased it will be necessary to use the half-halt frequently so this exercise must be well established.

Only from the combination of the impulsion and the half-halt will you start to achieve elevation which will only be for a step or two at first. You should then ride firmly forward in trot, making sure that rhythm is maintained. If you have difficulty in obtaining impulsion, an assistant on the ground may be able to help, but it is unwise to use someone with insufficient knowledge of the required rhythm and height.

Do make sure from the start that both hind legs work independently and evenly both in length of stride and activity. If you are doubtful at all, it would be best to get professional help.

It is always difficult to eradicate things that have gone wrong.

Question: I would like to teach my horse to passage, but do I have to do piaffé first?

Answer: You should try to establish piaffé first.

If you do it the other way round, then when you do come to piaffé the horse may try to use his passage steps, which will be too elevated for piaffé and cause considerable difficulty.

It will also probably be simpler to teach him passage from piaffé as this will have put his hindquarters well under him, putting him in a good position for more 'lift'.

However, it will be some time before you can do that as the transition from piaffé to trot must be well regulated first.

Question: I am told that my horse is 'nappy'. What exactly does this mean?

Answer: It means, basically, that he is doing as he likes, rather than being obedient to your aids.

There are so many ways in which a horse can be nappy, that I can only give a general answer.

Any question which you ask your horse, any movement or exercise which you want to do, should be obeyed instantly without resistances of any kind.

If the horse stops and refuses to go forward, kicks out, turns round, bounces on the spot, does not listen to aids and so on, then his behaviour constitutes napping.

It can be a big problem if the horse has been nappy for some time, as he is going to have to relearn to obey the aids. You may be in for quite a tussle which will involve a lot of determination to win on your part. You are going to have to use the aid of a whip to overcome the problems as the leg and seat will almost certainly be insufficiently strong.

Try and see it through if you can, as a napping horse is unpleasant to ride and, quite often, a danger to himself, his rider and others.

Question: My horse bucks and he often kicks out at the same time. Can you tell me if there is anything I can do to stop him?

Answer: It sounds as though he may not be bucking out of sheer high spirits, but as a resistance.

Horses find lots of ways of getting out of what we want them to do, and he may have discovered that if he bucks, humps his back or kicks out, he can get you out of the saddle, thus rendering you helpless at that moment.

If he is doing this, it is naughty and disobedient, and he should be smacked jolly hard with the whip so that he goes forwards. If he has really got into a habit, he may try to carry on bucking or kicking, and the only way out of it is to keep using your whip and be more obstinate than he is!

It may seem as if he will never give up, but I assure you he will if you are determined.

Bucking from high spirits or because the horse is too fresh is another matter. Try to lunge him for a few minutes before

42

you ride him if you think this is the cause and let him get some energy out of his system.

If he does do it while you are riding, pull his head up and ride him forwards, making him come more securely onto the aids. Then he won't have time to get a buck in!

Question: My horse seems to swish his tail a lot. Is this wrong?

Answer: A swishing tail is very often a sign that the horse is not happy in his work, he may be reluctant to do what you want or even 'nappy'.

There are degrees of swishing. An occasional swish may not mean very much, but a lot of activity or angry swishing could certainly be a resistance to the rider's aids. Generally it would be a dislike to the use of the rider's legs and so it would be necessary to teach the horse to accept the leg aids better.

The best way to do this would be to give the horse a sharp slap with the whip if he does not answer the legs willingly. As with all training the improvement may not be immediate, but, given time, and with perseverance it should get better.

Some swishing may be caused by anxiety, so do make sure that all aids are clear and exercises asked for are not too complicated for the horse's stage of training.

Question: I have a problem getting my horse past certain objects. They are not always the same things. He just decides not to pass something and will try to turn round or just before to go forwards. I have tried leading him past and using my stick, but nothing seems to help. Can you suggest anything?

Answer: You don't say how old the horse is. Youngsters

often do not want to go past new objects which they have not seen before, which is understandable.

It is wise to take an older reliable horse for company who can give a 'lead', so that this problem does not arise as, unfortunately, once a horse has discovered that he can get away with refusing to pass something he does not like the look of, it is then quite a nuisance.

Getting off and leading the horse past is really giving in to him. He has been asked to do something and even if he does not fancy the idea, he must learn to do as he is told. If you are alone this can be awkward but a firm line should be taken from the start.

If your horse won't go forwards from the whip and the aids, there is a serious flaw in your training. Horses must be made to respect the whip, in connection with the normal aids, from the beginning. They must be far more worried about upsetting their rider than any obstacle which they might meet!

Sometimes it may be necessary to 'sit out' a situation rather than entering into a confrontation, which the horse might win. Be prepared to stay all day to win the battle, rather than give in, as the horse will soon decide that he has the upper hand otherwise.

Question: When I am riding, I have noticed that my horse puts his tongue out of the side of his mouth quite a lot. Why does he do it?

Answer: This peculiarity is an evasion to the presence of the bit. It may originate from an injury to the mouth or the tongue itself, or it could be the result of a severe or badly fitted bit.

The horse may be making himself more comfortable due to the unsympathetic or restrictive hands of the rider. It can be a very difficult problem to correct, as the horse will develop the evasion to become a habit, and all habits are hard to cure. Proper use of the aids and improved submission to them will begin to correct the difficulty.

I have found that if these horses are made to go energetically forwards and the mouth kept alive by gentle, but active, action of the fingers, the horse has less time to think about this evasion.

Question: How can I stop my horse getting its tongue over the bit?

Answer: The horse is putting his tongue over the bit because he does not like the pressure of the bit; however, he has got to be taught to accept the pressure.

I think there are several things to try to do. First, fit the bit a little higher in the mouth than you would normally. Make sure it is not too wide as, if it is jointed, the centre will hang down too low and make it easier for the tongue to come over.

Next, use either a drop or flash noseband. This will help to keep the mouth closed which makes it less possible for the horse to get the tongue back. Ride the horse well forward into the hand and keep his mind occupied with answering the aids.

If the problem persists you could try using a tongue layer, but quite often the horse reverts to the evasion as soon as it is removed.

As a precaution it might be wise to have the horse's mouth checked over by the veterinary surgeon in case there is a physical problem.

Question: I constantly lose marks in dressage competitions because my horse comes 'above the bit'. I wonder how I can correct this?

Answer: Coming 'above the bit' is an evasion to the correct pressure of the bit in the horse's mouth. It may happen for a variety of reasons:

The rider may be failing to use the legs sufficiently to push the horse forwards into a contact.

The contact may be too hard or too loose for the horse to be able to accept.

The horse may be unhappy about the type of bit used or it may be badly fitted.

Insufficient preparation for a movement or sudden aids can cause the horse to fling his head up. Nervous or excitable horses are rather prone towards coming 'above the bit', unless ridden carefully.

Horses will sometimes come 'above the bit' if their balance is such that they feel the necessity to move the head and neck to 'save' themselves. They may actually be pulled 'above the bit', by poor riding, resulting from insecurity of the seat of the rider, who uses his reins for his own balance.

Good co-ordination of hands and legs will be important to the correction of coming 'above the bit'.

Question: I am told that my horse has a one-sided mouth. What does this mean?

Answer: It means that he responds to the rein aid on one side better than the other.

When the rein is taken, his mouth is softer to the hand on the side to which he will bend. It has probably come about by the rider being unaware of the importance of making the horse equally supple on both reins.

We often make our horses one-sided by being one-sided ourselves, using (a) inconsistent pressure to one side, or (b) constantly using a restricting pressure on one side.

Consider whether you come into either of these categories.

To correct the one-sidedness, work should be done on the harder side of the mouth to soften it, using flexions and correct bend.

In future a more equal use of the aids will prevent the mouth becoming hard on one side again.

Question: I have quite a lot of trouble with my horse crossing his jaw especially in downwards transitions. Why does he do it and how can I stop him?

Answer: Your horse is crossing his jaw as an evasion to the correct acceptance of the bit.

It will happen more in the downwards transitions if he is asked with more rein than leg. He will need to learn to accept the aids more evenly.

One exercise that will help to improve matters will be flexions to each side to loosen the jaw and poll which the horse may be using to aid his resistance. The flexion should be taken where the head joins the neck not further back. The horse should soften in his mouth to each hand before the other flexion is taken, the whole operation being done slowly and gently.

Force should not be used as it will result in more resistance.

Question: My horse seems to hold his head nicely and is very light, but I have been told he is 'behind the bit'. What does this mean?

Answer: If your horse is indeed 'behind the bit', then he is not truly accepting it.

This way of cheating the correct acceptance can be quite a big problem to correct if the horse has done it for some time. It sometimes leads to overbending where the horse evades even more by bringing his nose into his chest.

It can be quite a clever evasion and can fool the rider

because it feels light in the mouth. It is not until the horse is asked to do something more difficult, or to accept more impulsion, that the problem becomes apparent.

I think that the first thing to do is to make sure that your horse is going well forward from the leg. This energy should then travel through the horse and arrive at the front, then having to be controlled.

If the acceptance is correct the horse will take the bit and ask to go forward with his head and neck stretching towards it, not pulling or grabbing but allowing himself to be connected elastically. Any drawing backwards of the neck or nose will indicate that it is necessary to ride more firmly from the leg to create more impulsion.

Transitions will also be a help in improving this problem, but it will not be solved unless the rider maintains a firm contact, so that the horse learns not to avoid it.

Question: I am very worried because my horse has started grinding his teeth. Is there anything I should do?

Answer: If your horse has been working satisfactorily and has just begun to grind his teeth, it may be because he is worried about some new exercise which you are attempting.

If this is the case try to assess whether the work is too difficult at the moment, or whether you could make it easier by asking less for a few days. If you feel that you must pursue the exercise try to keep him as calm as you can, as grinding is usually caused by anxiety. Also, check that your aids are correct and clear. Once an exercise is fully understood, grinding will usually stop and, similarly, once the aids are fully accepted, the horse will relax and cease grinding.

Sometimes, unfortunately, the problem continues, or repeats itself with every new piece of work. This can be very difficult or almost impossible to correct, the horse having developed a 'habit'.

Question: I was schooling my horse one day and he suddenly twitched his ears quite violently and then did not seem to want to go forwards. Can you tell me why this might be?

Answer: There are times during training when this can happen. It could be to do with flies, which some horses hate more than others, but may be due to the difficulty of the exercise.

I think there are two main causes.

Any exercise requiring more bend, more impulsion or collection could cause some strain of the poll area. This could panic the horse or even cause it some pain. He reacts by ear twitching or even appearing to drop one ear lower than the other. It may last a moment or two, or even longer. The rider should immediately ease the pressure and ride more freely forward. After a few minutes the horse will relax and all will be well.

The exercise may be repeated but to a lesser degree for that day.

The second cause is over-restriction by the hands of the rider, in which case it will be necessary to learn to be more sympathetic.

Contact with the mouth should always be a 'feel' and 'ease' process, not a continuous grip.

One other word of warning regarding ears. It is very unwise to try to investigate for anything wrong inside the ear, as much damage could be done. If you are worried, do call in your veterinary surgeon.

Question: My horse never seems to have his ears forward when I am schooling. Is he bored?

Answer: Well of course he certainly could be! It depends what you are doing.

Schooling should not be boring to the horse if his mind is kept interested, and he is actually working. Riders should use school exercises intelligently, choosing some which are suitable to the horse's standard.

Work on an exercise until some improvement is made and then reward the horse by giving a brief rest on a long rein. Then work on the next exercise and so on.

Keep his mind alive by making him go forwards and by using the fingers to make conversation with the mouth. Try to avoid kicking him along which must be very boring for him. Also 'dead' hands are likely to kill interest in school work.

If the horse is learning and being rewarded for doing so, he will be more cheerful.

There are, I admit, a few horses that simply do not prick their ears however good their riders are, or however interesting the work may be. Fortunately they are in the minority, as I have found no real answer to this. They usually seem quite happy, and work well, but simply do not put their ears forward.

If you have one of these, he may not actually be bored, but just likes to carry them like that!

Question: My horse keeps tilting his head to the right. What can I do?

Answer: There can be several reasons for a horse to tilt his head. The rider's hands may be the cause.

Uneven contact, restricting, or hands too 'set' may make the horse unhappy enough to look for an evasion to the pressure of the bit. Incorrect training may cause tilting.

All through training the rider must be very aware of keeping his horse straight through the reins. If he allows stiffness to develop from poor use of the school exercises the horse will be less comfortable on one particular rein and tilting may result. Insufficient use of the legs to create energy into the bridle may cause the problem.

Sometimes there can be something wrong in the horse's

mouth such as a sharp tooth or, in the case of a young horse, changing teeth.

Whatever the cause, if the head continually, or occasionally, tilts, the normal procedure would be as follows:

Keep the contact on the side to which the nose tilts and use a feel and ease process with the fingers on the alternate hand.

After a while this should draw the head to an even position.

If the mouth remains hard on the side to which the head is tilting, an alternate pressure on each side of the mouth may help to achieve softening.

Firm use of the legs of the rider is essential to any correction.

Question: I have a lot of trouble with my horse shaking his head. What can I do to keep it still?

Answer: The first thing to discover is whether your horse is simply being resistant to the aids, which on the whole is usually the case.

It may take some time to find out if this is so, because teaching horses submission to leg and hand can be a lengthy process, particularly if the rider is a novice. Less knowledgeable riders take time to learn to co-ordinate their legs and hands, and unless their aids are correct and consistent, the horse may be slightly or even very, unsteady.

However, unfortunately, there are a few horses who suffer from head shaking due to a physiological problem. I know that there has been a good deal of research into this problem, but, to date, the solution has not been conclusive. I have known some head shakers to have been relieved or cured by treatment.

The very bad cases are a different matter and the best thing to do is to have veterinary advice. Such horses may be better employed in a sphere other than dressage where, although irritating, their behaviour cannot lose marks.

Question: I can't seem to stop my horse pulling. What do you suggest I do?

Answer: The first thing to do is to try to assess the reason for him pulling. There may be several, but the prime one could be lack of balance (on the forehand). For instance, he may use your hands to support himself, or lack of correct training will also cause pulling.

During training one of the first things to achieve is the establishing of a 'speed' in the horse's mind at each gait. Once he knows what is expected he will give up trying to go faster; pullers are often of impatient temperament trying to snatch the reins from the rider.

If they are taught to accept the aids: i.e. legs and hands for control, they will not be able to pull. Riders often make the mistake of 'pulling' back. This really can only aggravate the problem and, since the horse's strength is so much greater, is futile in any case.

Riders must achieve better control by learning the correct use of the aids, and how to put the horse 'on the bit'.

In the case of the horse pulling because he is on the forehand, the rider would need to know how and when to use a half-halt to correct the balance.

Some work done on the lunge with side reins can be a big help in teaching the horse to carry himself at a slower speed and therefore also a help when mounted.

Question: In trot my horse keeps putting me on the same diagonal. What should I do?

Answer: I believe that this problem occurs due to the one-sidedness, or stiffness of the horse.

A stiff horse normally has one side to which he curves willingly, and one to which he does not. The stride in the curved side will often be shorter, which will be less comfortable for both horse and rider, therefore the rider will probably automatically ride on the diagonal of the longer stride and often the horse will 'bump' a novice rider onto the diagonal which is best for him.

Try to improve the problem by disciplining yourself to change diagonals every ten strides or so, both to accustom yourself and to gradually even up the horse's muscles.

School exercises will in time make the horse more supple which will improve matters.

Question: Several times my horse has bolted with me. Can you tell me what to do?

Answer: Before I answer this question I think we should be clear as to exactly what bolting is.

It means to me that the horse is totally out of control, either from fright or because he is incorrectly trained. In this case he runs 'blind', not really knowing what he is doing, and may take the rider over or through any obstacle in his way, this being extremely dangerous.

If a horse escapes the aids for a short time, I would not class this as 'bolting'. The best remedy of course would be, never to allow it to happen! This may be easier said than done, but if you are careful, knowing what might set off the problem, it should be possible to avoid it.

As with most difficulties which occur with horses, the more obedient they are the better. This means patient training in teaching them to respect and answer the aids, preferably in an enclosed area, until they know that they must obey the rider. Then, even in a tricky situation out in the open, you will have a better chance.

Question: My horse has developed a nasty habit of rearing when he does not want to do something. What can I do?

Answer: Rearing is probably the most nasty evasion of all.

The horse has unfortunately discovered that by doing this he can get away from your aids and he has you at his mercy. There are ways of correcting a rearer which I really cannot go into in this book as they are best dealt with by very experienced riders. You may be forced to take him to someone to be 'sorted out', if you cannot overcome the problem yourself, and it should not be left too long either.

In the meantime, perhaps you should try going back to the beginning, and teach the horse the aids all over again. He must go forwards when told and this is the main thing to concentrate on. He will not be able to come 'on the bit' until he does, so get him to go forward at all cost and worry about the front end later.

Question: In a competition recently I was marked down because my horse was unlevel. When I enquired what this meant I was told he might have some trouble 'high up'. What did this mean and what can I do about it?

Answer: The term 'unlevel' is used when the stride is not quite even, either in front or behind. The horse can appear to be lame, at times, or possibly all the time.

'High up' is an expression used when the horse is unlevel behind and will refer to the possibility of there being something wrong in the back. This could be a fusion of two or more vertebrae due to arthritis or injury, or it could be a muscular problem. If it is the latter, it may be due to uneven development or a strain.

In the case of uneven development, better use of the training exercises correctly used, can improve or cure the problem, but it may take considerable time.

A strain is obviously a veterinary problem and should be dealt with accordingly.

In the case of fusion, which can be discovered by the use of X-ray, advice will again be given by the veterinary surgeon as to the horse's future use.